Here are poems that explore ... *, and always surprising, the intercon*... *l sky; body and soul; beast-howl and* ... *e and impermanence. These are poems that journey into rather than push against, and for this alone they are to be commended.*

—Alan McMonagle, author of *Ithaca* and *Psychotic Episodes.*

Jackie Gorman speaks softly as if her encounters with the natural world brought forth not a sense of dominion but kinship. Her hares, deer, birds are all looked at with the eyes of a true poet, slant, but aware too of the whatness of each creature, its habitat, its world. Sometimes this kinship leads her to slip her own skin and assume the habits of these others. But lest I give the impression that Gorman is some kind of quietist there is also steel here, clearest when she asks for her head to be shorn, with all the decisiveness of a woman sure of herself and her direction. These poems work like whispers on the mind, haunting and magical by turns.

—Dr John O'Donoghue, author of *Fools & Mad* and *Sectioned.*

Jackie Gorman understands nature and its healing embrace; here we have moving, sensuous poems that show a keen tenderness towards ageing parents as much as towards our island's native animals: hare, stag, badger, hedgehog, wolf. Birds, too, and water and dreamlike presences shadow these crafted poems. There is an ease to Gorman's pieces that disguises the muscular architecture of—and absolute care taken with—their composition. This is delicate, beautiful, strong work.

—Nuala O'Connor, author of *Becoming Belle* and *Miss Emily.*

Nature is a true source of inspiration in this accomplished first collection by Jackie Gorman. Her subject matter, animals and birds inhabit a world of observations and myth. Throughout the collection, Jackie Gorman is in search of a spiritual home. Her sense of freedom is evident from the start. She loves the shifting boundaries, the blur of light on water, the space between seeing and dreaming. Shape-shifter, in search of truth and permanence, Jackie Gorman has perfected that rare technique of creating poems, that insist you read and reread them.

—Noel Monahan, author of *Chalkdust* and *Where the Wind Sleeps.*

The Wounded Stork

poems by Jackie Gorman

Jackie Gorman

June,
looking forward to
Amergin! Jackie

Published by The Onslaught Press
19A Corso Street, Dundee, DD2 1DR
on 1 May 2019

ISBN: **978-1-912111-96-1**

The text is set in FF Celeste Book by Christopher Burke, and the back cover in Garamond

Printed & bound by Lightning Source On Demand Services

Place and a mind may interpenetrate
till the nature of both is altered

Nan Shepherd

Contents

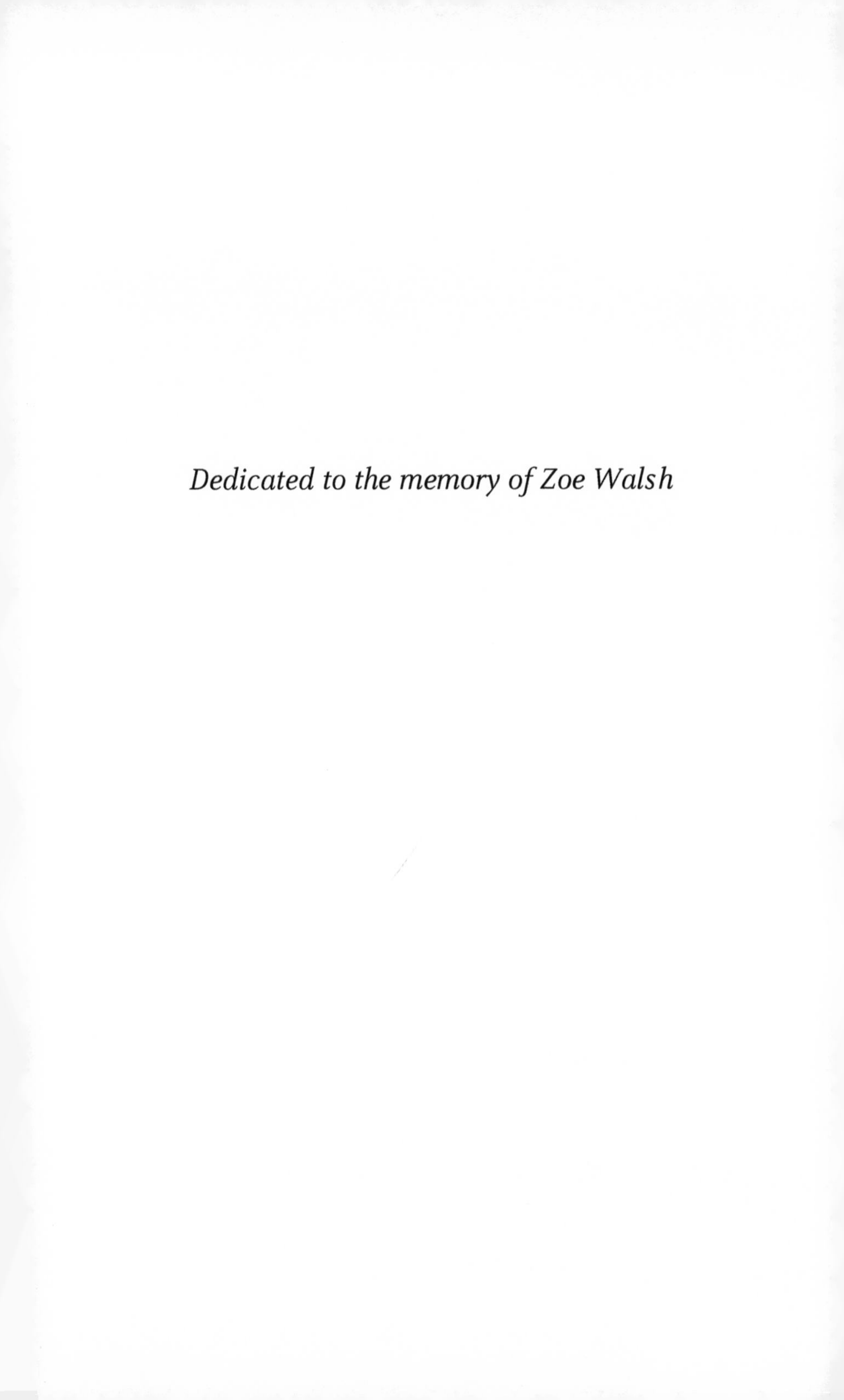

Dedicated to the memory of Zoe Walsh

Hypothesis

The word "crack" makes a sound, it makes us worry about what might be broken. It comes from the Old English word "cracian", which means to make a loud, abrupt sound. Even our voices may crack when we feel insecure or vulnerable. Yet like the light in a Georgia O'Keeffe painting, a crack may show a new spirit entering, the glimpse of something yet unknown. When something falls between the cracks, we may feel it is lost and yet it may open up a new space and in this we may catch a glimpse of a different light.

The Wounded Stork

Blackbird Days

A man swims and I watch his front crawl throwing light.
His body and tangled hair, shining in the lake shadows.

A blackbird flies across the stones, a blur of soot and fire.
My mind wanders and I watch the man in a daydream.

Dripping and smelling of the lake, he will take my car.
I will sit on the shore and wait for the light to change.

There will be a slow steady breeze, like a half-remembered tune.
The sound of the waves will seem tactile, like a baby at the breast.

When my mother answers the door, she will see this man with wet hair.
He will notice the geraniums and smell the badger in the hedge.

She will see the blackbird in his eyes and his open silent mouth.
Her mouth may open as if she's about to speak, but nothing happens.

And I having changed places with him, will move muscle and intuition
against the current, swimming into the waters out of reach.

Photograph of Water

The photograph was taken
the evening I drowned.
I am in the water just below the surface.
The lake is in a deep slumber
not woken by the pike
as it trembles through its dreams.
The rats sleep near the edge,
dreaming of ripe fruit and milk.
I can't say how old I am
as the water and light play tricks.
Look long enough and
you will see me floating.

The Wounded Stork

I

Some thought the birds changed into fishes when they disappeared for the Winter. They did not know that birds which weighed less than a cup of water could cross vast salty oceans. They wondered where they went and imagined birds turning into barnacles or mice or clinging upside down to trees. Aristotle suggested they went to the bottom of lakes and rivers, their weight as a flock bending the reeds and rushes, submerging the birds as one. He saw redstarts morph into robins in the Winter. Magnus told of ducks being born from a tree. Fishermen claimed that clumps of live swallows could be pulled from beneath the ice. Huge congregations of birds disappeared each Winter, swallows, cranes, thrushes and white storks.

II

The Rostock Stork flew from Africa with a brown arrow in its neck. Among its muster, crossing the Levant, it flew in darkness into the hush of the night's sky. The sound of the *Azaan* in its mind, the heat of the sun on its wings, the sap green light of the Taurus Mountains in its eyes. Shot in Germany, it became a Pfeilstorch, an arrow stork. Long broad wings designed to soar, its descent near Klütz, revealing migration, a strange word from the Latin *migrāre,* meaning to move. For a moment, it was so alive and shocked as it descended, like a caught fish returned to cold waters.

III

No more wintering grounds, it stands now forever trapped in the University of Rostock, behind smeared glass. So many people have reached out and tried to touch it and left a mark. It stands tall in a roomful of molluscs, fish and other birds. A glass case on a Cuban mahogany stand. Mahogany from *m'oganwo,* a word spoken by the people brought there as slaves, the Yoruba word for African mahogany trees. So much movement of words and people.

The Blue Hare

Stepping off the path,
a silver car rushes by.
I never saw it coming,
yet I felt the ground give way.
I knelt down within myself.

The hare that lives in my mind,
snug in her thick coat and
safe in her wide-open eyes,
breaks free and runs across me.

She purrs, sniffs my body,
looks up, pisses and moves on.
So it happens that I am reborn
into my warm russet fur and strong legs.

Mountain hare, white hare,
Irish hare, blue hare.
Many names, one thumping spirit.

A hare will not move until it has to,
stillness and camouflage its defence,
safe in its form of flattened earth.

What does it mean to be free?
Hare breath touching the ribs.
Watching everything going still,
galloping through swirls of thyme,
sedge and gorse.

An Giorria Gorm

Faoi choiscéim den teach
tiomáineann carr gheal faoi dheifir.
Ní fhaca mé ag teacht é,
ach baineadh croitheadh as an talún.
Téim síos ar mo ghlúine
i mo chroí istigh.

An giorria a mhaireann i m'intinn,
soiprithe ina cóta tiubh agus
sábháilte ina súile lonracha,
scaoileann sí saor agus ritheann sí tharam.

Crónaíonn sí, bolaíonn sí mo chorp,
breathnaíonn sí suas, múnann sí
agus bogann sí ar aghaidh.
Athbheirthe isteach i m'fhionnadh
donnrua te agus mo chosa láidre.

Giorria sléibhe, giorria bán,
giorria Éireannach, giorria gorm,
anam fuadach amháin.

Anáil ghiorria, lámh ar na heasnacha
ag fanacht go socair, cosa in airde
trí guairneán cuilithe de tím chreige,
clab chumhra agus aiteann.

The Acorn

Under the lamprey coloured sky,
you may find a single husk.
So small, you'll wonder why you noticed it.
Sterile, the life it once held devoured.
Warm it in your hands,
it will give a soft light and earthy scent.
It will twitch the noses of vixens and badgers.
When you put it down and walk away,
it may not be seen or held again.

Swimming Among the Stones

There isn't even a tree to hang my clothes on.
In this place of rock roses and hazel,
I want to swim.

There is no-one around.
So I go skinny dipping
in the scattered light.
Burning my back,
bobbing like a cork.

I emerge from the water,
as though from a dream.
My shoes have been washed away,
the flotsam and jetsam of memory.

I drive barefoot into Kinvara.
Exposed to the elements, scrubbed bare.
Like the landscape,
I have been karstified.

Water Memory

The bottom untouched by sunlight,
heart shrinking down
as though the future isn't real.
Nothing to hold on to.
Musty smell of the lake,
fish and forgotten hooks.
Boats on the horizon.
Just the water before thought.
My hook snagged in the want of this world.
A silent urge to be like water,
flowing yet strong enough to hold a ship.
In my notebook, I draw a fish.

Broken Light

Harebells stumble over limestone,
gulls scream in the brine-charged air;
a salty rush of wind and water
spills into the broken light.
At Cleggan, men twist freckled nets
in toughened hands.
Fish leap and scatter the sky,
one last wrench and the sea
freezes in their eyes.

The Nest

Among the mud and twigs,
I saw my father's death.
There was grey hair,
a walnut cardigan button,
a black pen and
a brain haemorrhage.
A clot, the colour of a fire engine.

Cow parsley drowned
in the clogged capillaries.
Shock, cold and indigo in colour,
bound to the heart.
The perfumed stench of impermanence
hung over the forget-me-nots.

A nervous bird with a red pointed beak—
the moorhen lingered near our house,
at the water's sunlit edge.

The Hare

Barney stopped the mower and looked down.
Full-grown, it was twitching in its soft fur.
I shivered when he mumbled "kinder to kill it."
With a mossy stone, he crushed it.
Its liquid eyes and long ears
stayed with me for weeks.

Lepus europeaus,
sacred to Eros,
shape-shifting woman,
Eostre's favourite animal.

I dreamt of it dancing in the callows,
when the moon was out.
Threading the faint light
between dusk and dawn,
thresholds of transition.

Barney limped,
next time I saw him
climb out of the tractor.

Shorn

Pale blue eyes looking up,
I put nitroglycerine under your tongue,
as we watch the football and
hum *Nessum Dorma.*
I help you to shave or tie a Windsor Knot,
each time noticing the beige circle
on your cheek,
melanoma erased by radiotherapy.

In July, you planted a rosemary bush.
Covered in ancient toil and sweat,
I help you undress in the hallway.
Closing the bathroom door, seeing you bare,
all of you was vulnerable and shorn,
shivering like a frightened lamb.
My skin burnt silently and slowly.

You looked at me and
I write you a poem with naked eyes.

The Hedgehog

My father lifted him
on a spade,
        placed him in the back field.
Years later, my mother
watched him
        scurry away.
I remember his tired eyes,
shedding spines ;
        he looked back
as if he knew she
        was following him
with her innocent eyes.

Twins

As you pushed into life,
I hid myself for 10 years in utero.
A face slowly carved out of water.
Now I smoulder inside you somehow,
waiting for a totally different life.

The Typewriter

I loved the sound of the punched keys
and the chime of the margin bell.
A heavy brown Adler on a small side table.
Saturday morning and Daddy's in the garden.
Mammy is gone to town since early.
Sometimes, I wonder aloud "why can't I go?"
I am writing a letter to Granny,
who is in the kitchen.

I rattle out words with a satisfying sound.
The letters are inky, **blurry** and **bold**.
Determined fingers push the black keys DOWN.
In the smudges, I can see myself.

The Collins Pocket Dictionary, 1902.

The red dictionary is restored,
the bookbinder smiling and hesitant.
The raised letters feel like a crust,
faded cerulean, the texture of memory.
Schoolboy pencil marks linger,
the cursive shames my scrawl.
I put it in my pocket and buy a new pencil.

Mary

In memory of Mary Murphy

The surface of the statue
is tarnished and cracked.
The pupils of your eyes are bright and sleek,
like the fur of a Syrian bear.

I wonder how it was for you,
after your son died.
All those misfits he hung out with
calling to your door,
looking for answers.
Some days you must have been tired,
just back from the market with dates
or cassia in your cal of palm leaves.

I think of you now
in the 15th century panel painting
by the Master of Erfurt.
Holding a spindle and thread,
your child the fabric of your body.

Grave Stone

I pick up a stone
from my granny's grave.
There she is.

The tweed and wool clothes,
the cursed Black and Tans
and the amber Rosary beads.

The turf and fires in the grate.
Frying eels with duck eggs.
Orange slices dipped in sugar.

My hand rubbing the
name on the headstone,
as if it were a raised scar.

Playing with Fire

For Bridget Gorman

She whispers the embers back to life.
The flames dance in the rusty grate.
An everyday ritual—making fire and watching.
Like Heraclitus, she believes
the soul is made of fire,
part spirit and part animal.
From this fire, a new place.

Wings

There will come a day when you will panic,
realising that you haven't seen what is happening.

Do not despair because then you will see your hands,
more than just fingers and a thumb, like a chimp.
More than ligaments and skin, like a knuckled starfish.

Your hands will fly up like two birds in flight.
There will be a flurry of sounds,
raucous caws of recognition.

For weeks, you will cough up quills,
barbs, scapi and hamuli,
everything you need to become.
You will piece all the parts together
with your knife-like beak.

You will dream of pecking out
the eyes of the dead,
smearing your skin with ant oil
and finding shiny treasures.

You become a dark angel shifting the soil,
a sable-plumaged spirit rowing through the sky.
The trees will rustle their incantations.
Your wings will suddenly be broken again
but this time, you remember you have claws.

The Wilderness

The fields and hedges went quickly,
swallowed up by new houses.
It closed her in and now
everything sounded different.

Her front door creaked like
a rasping corncrake.
A niece found her in the hallway
and said it was a heart-attack.
Warfarin every day, rat poison,
she wouldn't take.
Hawthorn and wild carrot
growing around her door.

Lightning

The unconscious doesn't waste much spit
telling you what you already know.
—Marie Louise von Franz

Something came to me last night
in the overcast moments before sleep.
It told me a truth, which I recognised
as my own, delicate and fragile.

I should have gotten up and
written it down. But it was late and dark.
I was tired. I thought I would remember.

Now I can only remember the
flash of light at the window.
I wasn't afraid, simply aware.
It's like that sometimes,
you are just too tired to open the window.

The Witch and the Astronomer

Katharina Kepler was accused of witchcraft.
Potions causing pain, an aunt who was a witch,
killing animals and turning into a cat.

Chained to a floor for 14 months,
threats of torture,
she would not confess
to what she had not done.

Her son Johannes abandoned
his celestial physics to defend her.
With a mind full of planetary motion,
he explained magic and she was freed.

I think of her now,
as I read stories of "the Salt Pit" in Afghanistan—
darkness, threats of rape,
captives chained to the floor.

Lies I've Told a Toddler Lately.

Teddy bears talk to each other at night.
All fish are called Nemo.
Your lovely eyes will fall out
from watching too much television.
There are fairies at the bottom of the garden.
If you are very quiet you might hear them.
The moon is looking right at you tonight so wave !
We are all kind to each other.
Books and toys get lonely too and it's ok to be sad.
I will always be here.

Persephone

In the Strand Book Store
in the East Village,
I searched for Persephone.

I found a hard-back book for $30.
I read it again and again
and then I understood.

She was acting out.
Demeter and Zeus had some faults as parents,
denying the nature of children to leave.

She loved the darkness,
the bitter-sweet taste of freedom
and pomegranate seeds.

She felt more fully alive,
emerging from the darkness
of the long Winter.

The Word "No"

Using the word "no" needs some rehearsal,
groaning it silently into mirrors,
making the shape of it with your mouth,
a poisoned heart-felt kiss.
Learning it in different languages,
sensuous and salty,
rolling off the tongue like an oyster.

When I see the sunlight, I will forget Icarus.
I will fly as close to the sun as I want to.
I will sing your name and the word "no".
I will see my feathers and the waves,
yet I will not curse my curious artistry.

Leda

The moon stares in the window
with skull-white eyes.
I hold my hands over my head,
as if comforting a child
or covering its ears.

Leda, Queen of Sparta.
I could not get you out of my mind.
My life blown away by
winds from the east.

Then I looked and saw
the shattered feathers on my pillow,
the shafts, vanes and barbs of a swan.

The Wolves of Chernobyl

Silent and spectral, the wolves of Chernobyl now eat
fruit and herbs.
They chomp down with their meat cleaver mouths on
black night-shade.
They enjoy its bitter taste after the juicy haunch of a deer.
Breathless from the speed of the hunt,
they barely notice the stubborn old women who refuse to leave.
The women now make Cherry Vodka for Christmas in a
radio-active forest.

Scientists tracked one wolf leaving the exclusion zone.
Its GPS collar broadcasted its last location,
before the battery died.
Then the wolf vanished from the map with a beep.
I dream of it still, eating foxberries and crab apples.
It seems unaware of the heritage it carries,
as it walks towards us with its cunning smile.
Yet, I welcome him warmly because he has endured.

The Easter Flower

The lily hangs its soft scent in the air.
It smells of purity, innocence and hope.
Alone with not even a leaf to hold it close.
It bursts from the tomb of the earth
for a sweet and short taste of freedom.
The young pregnant soil of Eastertime
pushes it forth.

People thought it sacred and some
called it the flower of resurrection.
I, as a Pagan, worshipped at its altar.
Seeking rebirth through its perfumed strength.

Blue Light

For Brendan Duffy

Blue, the colour of the heavens and the abyss.
Not so much a colour as a state of light.
No colour isolates itself so much.
It is the hue of horizons and seclusion.
Yet the word itself sings with memories.
Robin eggs, roofs in Autumn
blue with moonlight.
Cornflowers, sapphires and herons.
Endless liquid light
in which skies and dreams lie basking.

Haiku 1

in a long glass tube
he sees molecules scatter
days and sunsets known

Haiku 2

lather and razor
a sun yellow dressing gown
awaking mountains

The Gratitude of Corncrakes

For Catherine Casey

Crex, crex, the rasping sound of summer,
a shy bashful bird, its chestnut wings rarely seen.
Purple loosestrifes chase the moonlight.
Cream coloured eggs with rusty blotches lie in meadows.
Their destruction leading us to a strange and lonely place.

Murmuration

A breathing darkness,
a fast moving cloud.
Each bird dancing on the edge
of soaring and falling.
Swarming upon themselves,
thousands move as one.

I am filled with joy for an instant,
something infinite and fleeting.
Pareidolia, a pattern where none exists.
This must be like everything
we never get to say to each other.

Elephant Eye

Smelling their lumbering grace.
Seeing myself through an elephant's eye.
In the light, I can hear them breathing.

Watching elephants in the water,
glazed in brown-gold mud.
The American woman beside me smiles,
her face lights up like an acolyte
in an old religious painting.
Forgetting for a moment,
even the word 'elephant',
hearing only the warm grey herd moving.

No more hunting, no more logging or circuses.
They share infrasonic secrets.

I wonder what does the grass know of the elephant?
I hear a thud when I land hard in my own body.

The Glassblower

The glassblower has drawn
a whispering crowd.
In halting English he tells
us that until it cools
the glass is almost malleable.
We watch and wait and
hold our breath
and no-one makes a sound.

He is making a space
and we are all shimmering inside it,
his breath, his eyes as fluid
as the moving glass.
We see the shape
we want our lives to be.
The long slow rising love,
unbroken as it toughens.

Love and Synaesthesia

Colours are the deeds and sufferings of light.
—Goethe, THEORY OF COLOURS, 1810.

Pressing your hands to my spine, while God and my long-dead Grandmother sit silently watching. Smelling the colour of your hair, honey-yellow as an Autumn leaf-scape.

The clatter of the blood oranges from the market, which you hold in your hands. Nutmeg kiss and eyes blue with the sound of rain. I see the faintest whiff of mint oil in the air.

Hot sound of Czech sunshine; we kiss near the hawthorn hedge, 'hloh' in the tongue of your grandparents in the Sudetenland. A cloudburst of white flowers in my mouth.

Now, we clasp the wildness of cornflowers in our hands. Yet, when the heart is ready and ripe, a new path appears. I walk away slowly, collecting crow feathers and red stones.

Everything leaves a hint of what was, a noisy honeysuckle stain. My nose twitches and reaches out to this eerie scent. I taste the silence that I want my life to hold.

The Apple of Your Eye

I am an apple, waiting to hit the ground,
not wanting to be damaged or bruised.
Fragrant and fragile, you could smell
the stench of need from the street.
You strolled into the orchard
and you picked me.

I keep asking you to wash the stain
from your hand but it's impossible.
How could you keep it clean,
when you hold a whole heart
between your fingers?

You think you hear a whimper or a yelp.
Each sound unique,
with as many whorls
as a fingerprint.

The truth of things falls like snow,
silently and softly into your life.

The Ash Flower

After ASCHENBLUME *by Anselm Kiefer*

It was like looking into the
darkness for the first time,
fragile and eroding before my eyes.
Buttery radiance giving way to
blackened seeds.
I had gazed at it in books,
it drew me in every time.
Now, here it was in front of me.

I stood still for a long time.
Not fully understanding but knowing.
I dug into the painting with my eyes.
I thought it's the mutilation of memory.
In my mind I saw a tiny blackbird,
in German *gottling,* meaning little god,
a protector against lightning.

Then I saw it happen :
the oil, acrylics, clay, ash
and earth blended into one.

Aschenblume, an empty space
in a moment of transition
and I saw it happen.

Die Aschenblume

Nach Anselm Kiefer

Eine zerfallende Oberfläche mit Bläschen,
eine vertrocknete Sonnenblume mit ihren Wurzeln in der Luft.
Zuerst war es wie ein Blick in die totale Finsternis
Zerbrechlich und sich vor meinen Augen auflösend.
Ich hatte es in Büchern angestarrt.
Es hat mich in sich hineingezogen, jedes Mal.
Nun war es hier an der Wand vor mir.
Ich stand still für lange Zeit.
Nicht voll verstehend, aber wissend,
Anselm Kiefers Leinwand so nah bei mir.
Ich grub mich hinein in das Gemälde mit meinen Augen.
Für einen Augenblick glaubte ich,
meine Erinnerungen waren etwas getrübt.
Dann sah ich es geschehen.
Öl, Acryl, Lehm, Asche und Erde gemischt in einem.
Aschenblume, ein leerer Raum,
in einem Moment des Überganges,
und ich sah es geschehen.

The Chaffinch

This morning, outside the window,
a spink sang a tiny blessing.
Thomas Hardy told of these blinded birds
singing their song over and over again,
enduring and hoping through burnt eyes.

Air-pockets lace their tiny bones,
carving out space in flight.
Their song, a reminder that
what was and will be
can be taken from us in an instant.

Two Hyenas

You said my name and walked out to the back porch.
From the darkness they came near, their coats heavy and wet.
They howled, just before you said those things
you couldn't unsay.
A flash of lightning loosened the soil under the cashew tree.
Two hyenas chased each other around the tumbled earth.
A Mandinka woman at the market said
they brought the sun to warm the cold earth.
She said they can mesmerise with their eyes.
That loss of togetherness hits me now,
I think of your hands chasing mine.

Finding Yourself Alone

You are still waking up
and bumping into things;
doors, chairs and yourself.
Now, learn the language of alone.

Don't worry about tenses.
Like Hopi Indian,
alone is all present tense.
The division of time does
not exist in alone
or in the hot plains of Arizona.

Remember the Hopi woman
you met there one winter
and how she did things slowly.
Do one thing at a time.

You will remember being
warm, domestic and content.
You must be hungry again.
A hungry thing can become
anything it wants.

Anger

You remember the Renaissance painting you saw in Florence.

It was of the Seven Deadly Sins and there was anger
in the centre.
She was wild-haired and half-dressed in a flowing blue cloth.
She was astride a black boar, dappled in blood and light.
She waved a broad axe and you thought she was beautiful.

You wondered what happened to her.
You understand now that perhaps she had her reasons.

Horse Flesh

The smell of a burning horse
in a dream last night lingers.

Flesh grows over wounds with a vengeance.
In horses, it comes back darker and raised,
called "proud flesh".

Proud of the anger which says
a body belongs to itself.
Dark like a match, remembering
the moment before it was struck
and also the brightness of the flame.

Sometimes in the darkness,
you can see clearly.

Badlands

The badlands of the painted desert
with black velvet skies and
floating liquid birdsong.
There's the distant sound of dancing
being swallowed into the desert floor.
Muffled rhythms switch off
the beehive in my brain.
The hot silence says hold on,
like a dried up creek waiting for rain.
That is to say, let go of wanting,
endure but hold on, let go.
Rain is coming soon.

Chinese Lanterns

You knock on the door, just after he has left.
You say you've noticed I was upset.
You hand me a Chinese Lantern plant,
a gift from the Farmers' Market.

I thank you, noticing the delicate paper calyx
protecting the tiny fruits.
I don't ask you in and I close the door.
You pause for a second and move on,
like someone using a metal detector.

Later, when he comes home and asks
where the plant came from, I shiver.
My brain lights up like a Christmas tree.
He says "she should mind her own business."

In Japan, these tiny lanterns are used
to guide the souls of the dead.
I remember Charles Darwin said our
ancestor was an animal which breathed water.
I dream of walking into the lake,
towards the distant saffron light.

Weeks later, I notice how the plant grows
in the window light.
I thank you again and again.
I thank you still.

The Haircut

The day after my divorce,
I ask my hairdresser to shave my hair.
She asks me a lot of questions.

Are you sure?
Have you thought about this?
You might regret it.
Are you really sure?
You spent a lot of time growing it out.
Are you sure?

I realise she's asking me about something
I've already done.
I tell her to plug in the number 1 blade.

Field Notes—If Grief Were a Mammal

If grief were a mammal, its eyes would be large and hungry, like a bear at the end of Winter. It would often be hunted and fearful and because of this, it could turn on you in an instant. Its fur would not be sleek but tired and ragged.

On Summer days, it would swim beside you in the lake, shy and curious, gulping water in its broad muzzle. It would be self-aware because of a neocortex full of tricks—singing, scent-marking and using tools. The bones in its inner ear would transmit sound vibrations, so it would be able to hear the memories you would whisper. A single-boned lower jaw would give it a powerful bite, allowing it to cut and grind.

Oxygen-rich blood in its four-chambered heart would keep it strong. It would have breasts heavy with milk but no offspring to feed. This would cause you to write in your notebook with an exclamation mark—mammal from the Latin "mamma" meaning breast! How cruel is nature.

With its ursine warmth, grief would mostly be nocturnal. Street lights would let you admire the play of light and dark on its coat. Without you knowing, it would stalk you for a long time. It would smell you in the wind. It would have vulpine intelligence, feline agility and lupine strangeness. It would come to recognise you, even from a great distance. It would run to you, as soon as you approach. Hunger could be part of this apparent affection. No animal could ever be more faithful or devoted.

Not-Knowing

At night, dreaming of water and caged elevators,
the body's gentle war of independence.
A kind of self-becoming now fully known.
It is just being human and saintly at the same time.
What Freud called "the dark continent" coming into focus.
I wonder what Frau Freud thought of this.

Stumbling Stone

In Dresden, I step over a *Stolperstein.*
Dürerstraße 10, Altstadt,
here lived Sarah Altbach.
Born in 1882, murdered in 1938
in Occupied Poland.

In Nazi Germany,
when someone tripped over a stone,
they would say "a Jew must live here."
Eine Spur durchs Vergessen,
a trace against forgetting.
Naked branches reach up
towards the Saxon sky.

After Birth

I saw you as a fox cub,
warm in your own blood.
Eyes blue and in the future,
they would be amber.
Nestled in a den full
of whooshing and rhythm.
The wind takes you away,
you flow down like icy water.
I lurch forward with the
eyes and churning stomach of a vixen.

I remember the red heifer
two Summers ago, bedded down
in after-birth and hay.
The dead calf licked furiously clean.

Loss in every species has no words.
Yet, love lingers safe beneath the skin,
waiting for a chance to speak.

Wolves

I heard the rough magic of a wolf howl.
In our soft den in the Ore Mountains,
I listened as they circled outside.
Shades of white, ochre and umber,
long silver muzzles and flaxen eyes.
Baying sounds from older times,
the rapacious spoilers of innocence.
I felt them snuffling at our door and
I heard their low lonely whines.
You said the wolves wouldn't show themselves,
unless they were trying to tell us something.
I quivered and heard myself make
unfamiliar sounds that rendered us apart.
I thought of a Winter long ago,
your hands warm as fur.
My tired heart, thrown to the wolves,
wailing loudly through the fresh blue snow.

Pruning

Take your time, as if you are patiently waiting for someone.
Do not get distracted by beliefs or religion.
There is no need to think of pain.

Trees that need to be split to the bole are waiting for you.
But you have no axe, so pruning will have to do for now.

Choose a pruning saw with heat-treated teeth.
When it comes time, you'll know how to embrace
the cutting and the cuts.

Fajara Market

A maze of rough alleyways, muddy after the rains.
A Fula woman with a huge swollen eye,
illuminated suddenly in the sunlight.

The bruising is vermillion, like the dust from the Sahara on my car.
Dust brought here from the Tibesti Mountains
from rocks broken down by erosion and pulverisation.

A man selling caged canaries walks by with a flurry of twittering.
I see the Fula woman again, buying green tea and limes.
I think for a moment that she is caged too.

Moonlight Garden

When it comes to the punch, there's so little left to do,
and that tiny bit the heart has always known.
—Olav H. Hauge

I choose a tarot card called Justice.
I lock the door and I hang rosemary
and white feathers near the bolt.

I put away the old gin bottles, now full of rain.
Memories ooze like a clutch of trampled eggs.
The scattering dandelion clock tells the time.

I plant lavender for protection, under moonlight.
The crocuses close up their petals at night—
nyctinasty, a way to conserve energy.

I put on the blue dress with sugar skulls.
I find the knife my grandfather used
to cut through weeds
and I lay it down on the threshold.

The Lock

I remember swimming in the lake,
near Kriebstein, not knowing that
the stars which glittered above were
tiny knives in my back.
I close up.

Time and talking unpicks the lock.
It finds a heart like a tenement,
poor, crowded and neglected.
In this place, it finds a chick
left with an open wanting mouth,
as the songbird has left the nest.

Naming Things

The puzzlement on your face as I say the word “icicle”,
pointing out the “ice rocks in the fridge”,
you told me about a few minutes earlier.

Later, I ask you about Santa Claus
and how he travels,
trying to get you to say the word “reindeer”.

You can’t remember and
yet you leap up with delight,
like an elder at a naming ceremony,
naming someone for the first time—

“him fly in the snow.”
I can see him clearly
running through the sky
and the sadness when
I say the word “reindeer.”

The Cloonark Stag

Near the callows, I step out of my skin
and follow him through the trees.
Tawny antlers rise above the grass.
Spell of velvet coat, soft wet muzzle,
deep brown eyes.

He moves quietly and quickly,
knows where he's going.
I'd go anywhere with him
to follow the hazy scent of memory.
He has been here since the last Ice Age.

He does what he must to survive,
stripping the bark off ash and birch trees.
He may take something that doesn't belong to him,
kale or winter wheat, potatoes or rye.
Or perhaps what I want, another chance.

He shows me how to wait without waiting,
to notice everything and to see what I see,
digging up the soil with his cloven hooves;
the translation of something felt,
the dark deep silence where
we dream ourselves human.

My life reflected in his eyes, until I see I am him,
watching him slink towards my slough,
becoming its empty folds and creases.
I walk out of the woods and the clearing gleams.
Water and words, the trail I leave behind.
His breathing behind me, shallow and fast.
Here, see me as I am, dark crimson flesh, warm, solid.

Notes

The Wounded Stork

The term *Pfeilstorch* (German for "arrow stork") was given to storks injured by an arrow while wintering in Africa, before returning to Europe with the arrow stuck in their bodies. To date, around 25 Pfeilstorche have been documented. The first and most famous Pfeilstorch was a white stork found in 1822 near the German village of Klütz, in the state of Mecklenburg-Vorpommern. It was carrying an arrow from central Africa in its neck. The specimen was stuffed and can be seen today in the zoological collection of the University of Rostock. This stork was crucial in understanding the migration of European birds. The Rostock Stork in particular proved that birds migrate long distances to wintering grounds

The Witch and the Astronomer

In 1615, Katharina Kepler was accused of witchcraft in the German town of Leonberg. This accusation was based on the testimony of a neighbour Ursula Reinbold. She was defended by her son the astronomer Johannes Kepler in dealing with these accusations. At one point, she was imprisoned for 14 months and threatened with torture. It is estimated that approximately 50,000 people were executed as witches between 1500 and 1700.

Persephone

Persephone was the daughter of the goddess Demeter and she was kidnapped by Hades and later became the Queen of the Underworld. Demeter, in her misery became unconcerned with the harvest and famine ensued. Zeus commanded Hades to release Persephone to her mother. Because Persephone had eaten a single pomegranate seed in the underworld, she could not be completely freed but had to remain part of the year with Hades, and spend the rest of the time with her mother. The myth was often used by the ancient Greeks as a way to explain the seasons, the eternal cycle of the nature's death and rebirth.

Leda

Although time and poetry and art can represent the myth of Leda and the Swan with a veneer of romanticism, the myth has a primal form. Leda was the wife of Tyndareus, the King of Sparta and on the same day that she had sex with her husband, she was overpowered by Zeus when he took on the form of a swan which was been pursued by a bird of prey. She laid two eggs from which hatched four children. This is a rare phenomenon, heteropaternal superfecundation, fraternal twins who have different fathers. The children were Pollux, Castor, Helen and Clytemnestra. Helen and Pollux are considered to be the offspring of Zeus. Helen was the most famous of her children. "A legend tells how Zeus winged his wing to my mother Leda's breast, in the semblance of a bird, even a swan, and thus as he fled from an eagle's pursuit, achieved by guile his amorous purpose, if this tale be true. My name is Helen, and I will not recount the sorrows I have suffered." Euripides, Helen.

Haiku 1

This Haiku is about John Tyndall's research which explored the question which we have all asked as a child—why is the sky blue? He used a simple glass tube to simulate the sky, with a white light at one end to represent the sun. He discovered that when he gradually filled the tube with smoke the beam of light appeared to be blue from the side but red from the far end. Tyndall realised that the colour of the sky is a result of light from the sun scattering around particles in the upper atmosphere, in what is now known as the "Tyndall effect". He thought that the light scattered off particles of dust or water vapour in the atmosphere, like the smoke particles in the tube, but it's now known that the light scatters off the molecules of the air itself.

Tyndall knew that white light was made up of a whole rainbow of coloured light and thought that the blue light appeared because it was more likely to scatter off the particles. We now know that this is because it has a much shorter wavelength than red light and is much more easily scattered, so to our eyes the sky looks blue.

Haiku 2

This Haiku was written for Bloomsday 2018 and was part of an art installation by Nickie Hayden for the Bloomsday celebrations in the Olivier Cornet Gallery. It is now on permanent display in the James Joyce Centre. All of the Haikus in the installation were etched onto copper and placed on display for the audience to move and reposition, thus creating a different direction with each change. The collected Haikus created a living stream of consciousness which those attending the exhibition could inter-act with. My Haiku is based on the infamous opening scene where stately plump Buck Mullligan emerges to start the day and being a lover of classics intones Introibo ad altara Dei.

The Gratitude of Corncrakes

Corncrakes once common in Ireland are now a red-listed species. The bird is known for its distinctive grating call. Now they are only present in small numbers in north Donegal and western parts of Mayo and Connaught. This decline is due in most part to intensive farming practices, including early mowing to make silage and mechanised hay making practices which have destroyed nests and driven corncrakes from old habitats. In a conversation about corncrakes and ecology in general with ecologist Catherine Casey about how increasingly everything has to have a monetary value, she made a remark about some things being priceless like having "the gratitude of corncrakes." I wrote it down because I loved the expression and also what it communicated about our relationship to the natural world.

Love and Synaesthesia

Synaesthesia is a perceptual phenomenon in which stimulation of one sensory or cognitive pathway leads to automatic, involuntary experiences in a second sensory or cognitive pathway. Synesthetic associations can occur in any combination and any number of senses or cognitive pathways. The term is from the Ancient Greek σύν syn, "together", and αἴσθησις aisthēsis, "sensation". The interest in coloured hearing dates back to Greek antiquity, when philosophers asked if the colour (chroia, what we now call timbre) of music was a quantifiable quality. Isaac Newton proposed that musical tones and colour tones shared common frequencies, as did Goethe in his book *Theory of Colours.*

The Ash Flower

Aschenblume [1983-97] is a painting by the artist Anselm Kiefer. It is on display in Modern Art Museum of Fort Worth, Texas. In the painting he explores the tensions in national identity through Nazi imagery and symbolism. The work depicts the grand Mosaic Room in the Reich Chancellery, Berlin, designed by Albert Speer. It recedes into space and Kiefer blurs the image by covering the surface of paint and emulsion with ash. The space is empty, except for a tall dried sunflower plant. In this painting, Kiefer uses unconventional materials to suggest processes of transformation. In this case, he suggests a space in a moment of transition, in which new images can grow from the brittle goals of the Third Reich.

The Chaffinch

The chaffinch was once a popular caged bird and often competitions were held where bets were placed on which caged chaffinch would repeat its song the greatest number of times. The birds were sometimes blinded with a hot needle in the belief that this encouraged them to sing. Thomas Hardy wrote a poem about this practice and in it, he contrasts the cruelty of blinding the chaffinches with their joyous song.

Not-Knowing

Michel Foucault warned that the disciplining practices of the nineteenth century with regards to women's sexuality had constructed sex as "a problem of truth". He said "What was once taken to be ordinary knowledge of women's more robust sexuality and her greater orgasmic capacity submerged into the mire of ignorance." Freud referred to women's sexuality as a "dark continent" for psychoanalysis, using colonial explorer Henry Morton Stanley's description of Africa.

Stumbling Stone

A *Stolperstein*, literally meaning "stumbling stone" in German is a concrete cube bearing a brass plate inscribed with the name and life dates of victims of Nazi persecution. The stones are placed at the place where the person lived and to date, they have been laid in 22 countries. The German word *Stolperstein* is sometimes used as a phrase to describe a "potential problem". It can also mean to find out something by accident. In this way, the word invokes the anti-Semitic language of the past and provokes a discussion about how we use language. Stolpersteine are not placed in obvious places and are often only noticed when you are very close to them. This is in stark contrast to museums and memorials which are deliberately visited and can also be easily avoided. According to the artist Gunter Demnig, Stolpersteine represent a much deeper intrusion of memory into everyday life.

Thanks and Acknowledgements

For support, encouragement and inspiration, thanks and acknowledgements to the following people. Noel Monahan, Eleanor Hooker, Brendan Duffy, Nuala Ní Chonchúir, Alan McMonagle, Colm Keegan, Dr John O'Donoghue, Gabriella Attems, Thomas McCarthy, Helen Ivory, Kerrie O'Brien, Dr John Lavin, Dr Michael Hinds, Jane Clare, Dr Jim Flannery, Gearoid O'Brien, Ivan Molloy, John Robinson, Catherine Casey, Mary Holahan, James O'Leary, Heather Brett, Angela Carr, Liz Warren, Matthew Staunton, Pól Ó Colmáin and Máire Logue.

Thanks also to the wonderful spaces and opportunities provided to me by the Tyrone Guthrie Centre, Listowel Writers' Week, Poetry Ireland, Cill Rialag Writers Residency Programme and The Arts Office, Westmeath County Council.

Previous versions of some of these poems have been published in the following publications—*Poetry Ireland Review, Obsessed With Pipework, The Galway Review, The Phizzfest Awards,* T*he Listowel Writers' Week Awards, The Lonely Crowd, The Sow's Ear Poetry Review, The Blue Nib Chapbook 1* and *Anthology, The Windows Anthology, Can You Hear What I See?, Respond, The Honest Ulsterman, Tales From The Forest, Headspace, Wordlegs, The Sentinel Literary Quarterly, Bare Hands, The Lakeview International Journal of Arts & Literature, Poet Head, Boyne Berries, Ring Around The Moon, Headstuff, Scáthán, Studies in Arts and Humanities* and in a Bloomsday 2018 Exhibition by artist Nickie Hayden.

Biography

Jackie Gorman has been published in a number of journals including Poetry Ireland Review, The Lonely Crowd, The Honest Ulsterman and in anthologies such as The Windows Anthology. She was part of the 2017 Poetry Ireland Introductions Series, a national programme to profile and support emerging poets in Ireland. In the same year, she won the Listowel Writers' Week Single Poem Award and was commended in the Poem of the Year Award at the Bord Gáis Energy Irish Book Awards. She has also been commended in the Patrick Kavanagh Poetry Awards. She has recently completed a Masters in Poetry Studies at Dublin City University.

Lightning Source UK Ltd.
Milton Keynes UK
UKHW011302310120
357953UK00001B/43